John Burgoyne

British General

Colonial Leaders

Lord Baltimore
English Politician and Colonist

Benjamin Banneker
American Mathematician and Astronomer

Sir William Berkeley
Governor of Virginia

William Bradford
Governor of Plymouth Colony

Jonathan Edwards
Colonial Religious Leader

Benjamin Franklin
American Statesman, Scientist, and Writer

Anne Hutchinson
Religious Leader

Cotton Mather
Author, Clergyman, and Scholar

Increase Mather
Clergyman and Scholar

James Oglethorpe
Humanitarian and Soldier

William Penn
Founder of Democracy

Sir Walter Raleigh
English Explorer and Author

Caesar Rodney
American Patriot

John Smith
English Explorer and Colonist

Miles Standish
Plymouth Colony Leader

Peter Stuyvesant
Dutch Military Leader

George Whitefield
Clergyman and Scholar

Roger Williams
Founder of Rhode Island

John Winthrop
Politician and Statesman

John Peter Zenger
Free Press Advocate

Revolutionary War Leaders

John Adams
Second U.S. President

Samuel Adams
Patriot

Ethan Allen
Revolutionary Hero

Benedict Arnold
Traitor to the Cause

John Burgoyne
British General

George Rogers Clark
American General

Lord Cornwallis
British General

Thomas Gage
British General

King George III
English Monarch

Nathanael Greene
Military Leader

Nathan Hale
Revolutionary Hero

Alexander Hamilton
First U.S. Secretary of the Treasury

John Hancock
President of the Continental Congress

Patrick Henry
American Statesman and Speaker

William Howe
British General

John Jay
First Chief Justice of the Supreme Court

Thomas Jefferson
Author of the Declaration of Independence

John Paul Jones
Father of the U.S. Navy

Thaddeus Kosciuszko
Polish General and Patriot

Lafayette
French Freedom Fighter

James Madison
Father of the Constitution

Francis Marion
The Swamp Fox

James Monroe
American Statesman

Thomas Paine
Political Writer

Molly Pitcher
Heroine

Paul Revere
American Patriot

Betsy Ross
American Patriot

Baron Von Steuben
American General

George Washington
First U.S. President

Anthony Wayne
American General

Famous Figures of the Civil War Era

John Brown
Abolitionist

Jefferson Davis
Confederate President

Frederick Douglass
Abolitionist and Author

Stephen A. Douglas
Champion of the Union

David Farragut
Union Admiral

Ulysses S. Grant
Military Leader and President

Stonewall Jackson
Confederate General

Joseph E. Johnston
Confederate General

Robert E. Lee
Confederate General

Abraham Lincoln
Civil War President

George Gordon Meade
Union General

George McClellan
Union General

William Henry Seward
Senator and Statesman

Philip Sheridan
Union General

William Sherman
Union General

Edwin Stanton
Secretary of War

Harriet Beecher Stowe
Author of Uncle Tom's Cabin

James Ewell Brown Stuart
Confederate General

Sojourner Truth
Abolitionist, Suffragist, and Preacher

Harriet Tubman
Leader of the Underground Railroad

John Burgoyne

British General

Daniel E. Harmon

Arthur M. Schlesinger, jr.
Senior Consulting Editor

Chelsea House Publishers

Philadelphia

CHELSEA HOUSE PUBLISHERS
Editor-in-Chief Sally Cheney
Director of Production Kim Shinners
Production Manager Pamela Loos
Art Director Sara Davis
Production Editor Diann Grasse

Staff for *JOHN BURGOYNE*
Editor Sally Cheney
Associate Art Director Takeshi Takahashi
Series Design Keith Trego
Cover Design 21st Century Publishing and Communications, Inc.
Picture Researcher Pat Holl
Layout 21st Century Publishing and Communications, Inc.

The Chelsea House World Wide Web address is
http://www.chelseahouse.com

First Printing
1 3 5 7 9 8 6 4 2

Library of Congress Cataloging-in-Publication Data

Harmon, Daniel E.
    "Gentleman Johnny" Burgoyne / Daniel E. Harmon.
        p. cm. — (Revolutionary War leaders)
    Includes bibliographical references and index.
    ISBN 0-7910-6390-9 (hc : alk. paper) — ISBN 0-7910-6391-7
    (pbk. : alk. paper)
        1. Burgoyne, John, 1722-1792—Juvenile literature. 2. United
    States—History—Revolution, 1775-1783—British forces—Juvenile
    literature. 3. Generals—Great Britain—Biography—Juvenile litera-
    ture. [1.Burgoyne, John, 1722-1792. 2. Generals. 3. United States—
    History—Revolution, 1775-1783.] I. Title. II. Series.

    DA67.1.B8 H374 2001
    973.3'41'092—dc21
    [B]   2001028519

Contents

The fireworks display was held to celebrate England's victory at the end of the Seven Years' War between France and England. The war lasted from 1756 to 1763.

A "Gentleman" Soldier

He was known as "Gentleman Johnny" to British soldiers and noblemen alike. He was smart, attractive, and fun-loving. But in a way, he was unlike some of the other young Englishmen at that time who claimed power and social standing simply because they came from wealthy families. Johnny Burgoyne cared about the basic well-being of others. As a result, almost everyone liked him. Common soldiers, or **redcoats** as they were called, who served under him in war respected him more than most other officers.

Johnny was born February 4, 1722, in Sutton,

near London. His father, also named John, is believed to have been a British army captain.

The youngster received a first-class education at Westminster School. He especially enjoyed Greek and Roman classical literature. Johnny grew to be handsome and tall, attracting the attention of many young girls. He made friends with the most respected English families.

At 15, he joined the army. Rich young men during those times could expect to become army officers at an early age, if they chose. For Johnny, the army would become one of several careers in his life.

One of his young friends was Lord Strange, whose father was the Earl of Derby. While still a teenager, Johnny fell in love with the earl's daughter Charlotte. He persuaded her to run away with him and get married in 1743. Not surprisingly, the earl was furious. He refused to support the young bride and groom, or even to see them.

Johnny's army career was progressing nicely,

though. Thanks to his family connections, Johnny was made an officer in the 1st Royal **Dragoons**. In the 18th century, an officer's **commission** was a valuable title. Wealthy officers who didn't want to fight often sold their commissions to eager young men.

Soon, Johnny was forced to sell his commission and leave the army because of his careless lifestyle. He played cards regularly and made wild bets. In the early years of his marriage he faced financial ruin due to his gambling. The couple went to live in France to avoid paying their debts.

For several years, Johnny and Charlotte struggled to get by. At last, her family forgave them. They even bought Johnny a new army commission, this time as a captain in the 11th Dragoons.

This time, he was mature enough to focus on his career. He drilled his men until they earned a reputation as one of the sharpest fighting units in the Royal Army. They even caught the notice of King George III. They became known as

Burgoyne's Light Horse. King George later gave them a very special name: the Queen's Light Dragoons. "Gentleman Johnny," as his troops nicknamed him, became a court favorite.

He also was becoming a favorite of London society. He bought the finest dinners and wines and entertained his friends often—an expensive way of life. When he later went to war, he continued this lifestyle.

In 1756 events in Europe started a war that would take Johnny away from his life of leisure. The Seven Years' War was a massive conflict, with far-ranging effects.

It was actually a "world war." It pitted those two old rivals, England and France, against each other. Many other nations also were involved. Joining England's side were two German states: Prussia and Hanover. Allies of France were Russia, Austria, Sweden, Saxony, and Spain. Battles were fought across Europe and in two far-off lands, India and America.

The Austrians, Prussians, and other countries

The Thames River runs through London. The river was important to England as a source of drinking water and as a way to transport goods. Several bridges connect the northern and southern parts of London.

had various reasons for going to war. As for England and France, the big argument was over control of lands in India and America.

The war began with Prussia's **invasion** of Saxony. As its name suggests, the war lasted seven years, until 1763. The English and Prussians were the big winners. Among other gains,

King George III expected the American colonists to follow the laws and pay the taxes imposed by Great Britain. The king would call on Johnny to use his skills in fighting the American colonists.

England claimed a larger share of the overseas territories, or **colonies,** than France. Naturally, France was unhappy with the result. This long-standing feud with England was the reason

France would become a friend of the American rebels 15 years later.

Johnny was 34 years old when the Seven Years' War began. He served in France, then earned his first real measure of fame in 1762 in Portugal. There, he led 3,000 troops in overpowering a Spanish stronghold at a town called Valencia d'Alcántara on the frontier between Spain and Portugal. His feat brought cheers both in Portugal–whose king presented him with a diamond ring–and in England.

Meanwhile, he had won an important post in government. Johnny was both a fine writer and public speaker. He was elected to the House of Commons, a part of the British **Parliament**, in 1761–although he couldn't occupy his seat in Parliament until he returned to London at the end of the war.

Johnny enjoyed his role in the British government and the prestige and power it gave him. He was reelected to Parliament in 1768. One of the matters under debate during his years in government was setting rules of foreign trade by the British East India Company. Johnny played a part in getting an important law passed called the Regulating Act. In most matters debated in Parliament, Johnny sided closely with the interests of King George.

Tragedy struck in 1764, when his 10-year-old daughter Charlotte Elizabeth died. Except for this period of grief, though, Johnny was content living in peacetime England. He became known for his poetry and other writings. At the same time, his personal fortune was made secure by his wife's large inheritance and his appointment as governor of Fort William in the northern part of England.

He also was becoming more and more popular in England's high society. He continued to play cards, dance, and dine with the members of the British upper class. And he earned recognition as a **playwright**. His first play was performed in 1774. Titled Maid of the Oaks, it was well received by theatergoers.

Prussia joined with England in fighting France and its allies in the Seven Years' War. Prussian army camps were well organized, as can be seen here.

Johnny fully enjoyed this life as a "gentleman" in London. But the time was approaching for him to become a soldier again. He yearned for adventure, and the army would soon provide him with the opportunity to serve his country again.

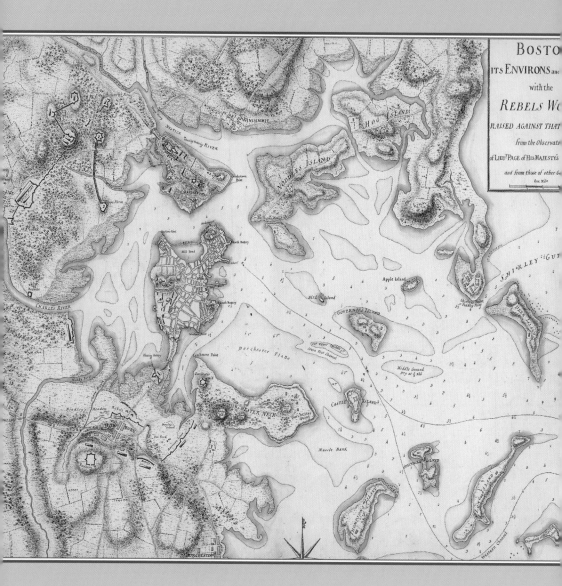

Johnny was promoted to major general and was sent to Boston, shown on this map, to fight in the American Revolution.

Off to America

In May 1775 the government in England was unhappy with the way things were going in the American colonies. Rather than give in to Britain's taxes and demands, the colonists were rebelling. They actually had fought **skirmishes** against the king's troops in Massachusetts. Now they were forming a sizeable army.

By now, Johnny had been promoted to the rank of major general. The military command decided to send him to the colonies with two other well-known British generals, Henry Clinton and William Howe.

This was an exciting time for Johnny. Perhaps here he would earn not just more credit as a talented army commander, but a place in history as a conquering general. More likely, though, he imagined he was being sent on a mission against a weak, disorganized opponent. The American "rabble in arms," as he called the rebels—most of whom didn't even have uniforms—probably would have thrown down their arms and given up by the time he got there.

The three experienced leaders arrived with fresh troops in Boston. There, a redcoat army under the command of General Thomas Gage was under **siege** by a large **Patriot** force. Only weeks before, the American Revolution had begun with the exchange of rifle fire at Lexington and Concord, Massachusetts.

"Gentleman Johnny" Burgoyne, Clinton, and Howe found the army at Boston in a dreadful mood. The British had never expected to be cooped up by the **homespun** colonial rebels they despised. The British were the ones who should be in control, marching freely through New England, crushing Americans strongholds and capturing and hanging rebel leaders. To their surprise, the Patriots had turned the tables.

Gage was encouraged by the arrival of the three younger generals and their troops. Together, they made plans to push forth from Boston and defeat the Americans.

In the coming months, Johnny commanded the British **artillery**

The armies that marched across the American colonies during the Revolutionary War consisted not only of soldiers, but also of **civilians**. Wagoneers drove teams of horses pulling supplies. Merchants set up portable tent stores to sell equipment and clothing, as well as items like tobacco to provide a few simple pleasures.

Many of the "camp followers" were women. Historians estimate as many as 2,000 women and children went along on General Burgoyne's 1777 campaign into New York. Some were soldiers' wives and girlfriends. Others were women who cooked and washed clothes for the army.

One of Johnny's best officers, the German Baron Friedrich von Riedesel, took his wife, three small children, and family servants with him to America. Baroness von Riedesel's letters gave historians valuable details of the Saratoga campaign.

against the American army that surrounded Boston. To some Revolutionary War historians, he played only a minor role here. He was just another British officer grasping for the right moment in history to win military glory.

He learned important lessons in these early days of the Revolution, though. There was plenty of fighting. British soldiers attacked the American position on Breed's Hill. This became known as the famous Battle of Bunker Hill. It was a long, costly fight. Eventually, the Americans were driven back. But they had inflicted heavy losses on the British. Almost 2,000 redcoats—40 percent of the British army—were wounded or killed. Another "victory" like that one, General Clinton said, "would have ruined us."

In a letter to England, Johnny described the fighting and the bombardment by artillery. He painted a frightening picture of "the roar of cannon, mortars, and musquetry; the crush of churches . . . and whole streets falling together in ruin."

The Battle of Bunker Hill took place on June 17, 1775, in Charlestown. The British army pushed the Americans back and claimed victory. Many British soldiers died in the battle. John would use the lessons he learned here later in the war.

Johnny had seen the problem plainly: The Americans had been well entrenched. British infantrymen had charged across an open field against lines of enemy riflemen who were protected by earthworks. Rather than send unprotected foot soldiers against such strong defenses, Johnny realized, the solution was to pound the enemy trenches with cannon fire. His goal was to kill most of their soldiers, or drive them back from their trenches, before sending in the infantry.

Two years later, along Lake Champlain in New York, Burgoyne would use the wisdom he obtained at Breed's Hill. He would insist on heavy artillery attacks before sending in the troops.

The British leaders saw that this rebellion in the colonies would not be put down easily or quickly. "Gentleman Johnny" had not been sent on a meaningless sporting trip after all. He was in for a real war—much to his satisfaction.

After Breed's Hill, the British took no significant action for a long time. They stayed in Boston, forming their plans and waiting for more soldiers from England. Not until the next year did they begin their attack in earnest.

General George Washington is shown here taking command of the American army in Massachusetts in 1775.

By then, George Washington would be the Americans' commanding general. Gage would be replaced in New England by General Howe. And where would Johnny Burgoyne be? His wife had died while he was in America. Looking beyond his personal grief, he focused on his army career. There was a war to win, and glory to be gained.

King George ordered the British commander in Boston, General Thomas Gage, to return to England in October 1775. Johnny was not sad to see him go. Johnny considered Gage a poor army leader. If Gage hadn't been so slow to act, the British might have seized control of the situation around Boston and ended the American uprising before it ever got started. That was Johnny's belief—and he said so in letters he wrote to powerful men in London. Those men valued his opinion. His criticism in part led to Gage's recall.

He wasn't especially happy with Gage's replacements, either. The crown decided to divide command of British forces in the colonies. General William Howe would direct operations in America, while the governor of Canada, Guy Carleton, was given command of the king's Canadian army.

The military leaders in London assigned Johnny to serve as Carleton's second in command with the Canadian army. He was to take a force of soldiers from the regular British as well as **Hessians**–German units fighting for England–to join the large army of Canadians whom Carleton already had assembled.

In May 1776, Johnny joined Carleton in Canada. Together they moved southward down the Richelieu River toward New York. They had an army of about 13,000 regular soldiers, plus **Tories** and Indians friendly to the British cause. This should have been more than enough to push victoriously to Albany, crushing any Patriot **militia** army that got in the way.

Something unexpected got in the way instead. On Lake Champlain, a 125-mile-long body of water between Montreal and Albany, American shipbuilders were constructing a fleet of warships. If left unchallenged, they could hamper any British movements between New York City and Canada. The American naval unit on Lake Champlain, Carleton decided, must be destroyed.

Carleton stopped his expedition and ordered the building of a British naval force on the lake. In three months, it was ready to sail against the Americans. On October 11-12, the British fleet attacked the American ships of Benedict Arnold. The Battle of Valcour Island was long and costly for both sides. Finally, the British prevailed. One by one over a period of two days, the American ships were battered and sunk.

Winter's chill by now was in the air, however. Carleton was afraid to continue southward unless he could be certain his mission would be accomplished and his army warmly quartered before snow and ice gripped the region.

After struggling over his next course of action for several weeks, Carleton decided to withdraw his great army to Canada for the winter. This made Johnny angry. It meant that although the British fleet had beaten the Americans on Lake Champlain, the invasion of New York had failed, at least for 1776.

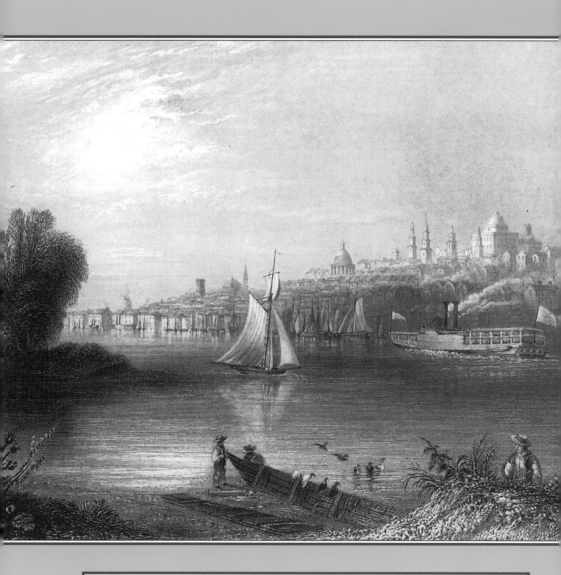

Johnny moved his troops from Canada to upstate New York. He thought he could end the American rebellion by attacking the Patriots in Albany.

3

Johnny Commands an Army

Although he questioned the qualities of some of his fellow generals, "Gentleman Johnny" had great confidence in the British army— and in himself. He arrived back in London in December for the winter of 1776-77. There, he made a bold bet with Charles James Fox, a close friend of his in Parliament. By the next Christmas, Johnny predicted, he would defeat the rebels and return to London as a hero.

His friend happily accepted the bet. Fox knew little of life in the colonies or of the American spirit of independence. But he knew any major army

While Johnny spent the winter of 1776-77 in comfort back home in London, the common British soldiers stayed in "winter quarters" in America. They found the best shelter they could—occupying colonists' homes and public buildings, if possible. Many had to live in crude farm buildings and frontier shelters, trying to avoid the blasts of sub-freezing winds that howled down from Canada and across the icy Great Lakes. Some died from sickness; others lost toes and fingers to frostbite.

They managed to have fun on occasion, though. Lieutenant James M. Hadden, one of Johnny's artillery officers, wrote in his diary that the soldiers sometimes went ice skating on the frozen lakes and rivers.

campaign would take a long time to organize and carry out. Even if the Americans were easily beaten, as Johnny anticipated, it was unlikely this could be accomplished soon. To James Fox, it seemed like he would easily win the money from the bet.

Johnny believed that if he were the commander of the Canadian force, he could carry out the New York invasion and hasten the war to its end. At this point, a very important person in London agreed with him: Lord George Germain, the king's secretary of state for the colonies. Germain was the person who decided which British generals would command which armies in America. Happily for Johnny, Germain did not like Canadian Governor Carleton. During his winter leave, Johnny had a favorable meeting with Lord Germain and King George III.

He had a plan for success–a good one. He wrote a paper titled "Thoughts for Conducting the War from the Side of Canada." It was similar to the previous plan for a divided attack on the upper colonies, but with improvements. Johnny wanted to organize a force in Canada and move down from Montreal, along the Richelieu and Hudson rivers and Lake Champlain, into the colony of New York. A vast army led by General Howe would march upriver from the port of New York. A third force, made up mostly of Tories, Indians, and Hessians, commanded by Lieutenant Colonel Barry St. Leger was to come eastward through the Mohawk River Valley from its base on Lake Ontario.

After crushing all resistance in their broad paths, the three armies would meet at Albany.

The rebellion in the north would be defeated, and the New England colonies would be cut off from those in the south. The lower colonies undoubtedly would have to lay down their arms quickly.

In May 1777, Johnny was back in the Americas —where his British troops had spent the winter in much less comfort, fighting frostbite and sickness. He had the pleasure of hand-delivering a letter from Germain to Carleton in Quebec. In it, Germain divided the Canadian troops. He left Carleton in command of a Canadian "home" army—but it was a small force of only several thousand men. Germain placed Johnny in command of the much larger army that was to renew the invasion of New York.

Johnny finally had what he'd wanted for a long time: field command of an army powerful enough to affect the outcome of the war.

Johnny was a firm believer in the British cause in America. He considered the rebels to be stubborn and worthless. He described their idea of self-government as a "system of tyranny." As for their army, it was nothing but a "preposterous parade of military arrangement."

He moved his force southward into what is now upstate New York in June 1777. In announcing the goal to his troops, he emphasized: "This army must not retreat." Meanwhile, he issued a plea to **Loyalists** in the region—colonists who remained loyal to King George. Johnny begged them to take up arms and help the British army put down the Patriots. Many Tories were more than willing to do just that, but would they be enough to help Johnny succeed in his invasion?

A more important

When General Burgoyne set forth to conquer the Patriots in New York in June 1777, the first part of his expedition was by water. His army and supplies were carried southward from Canada along the Richilieu River and Lake Champlain by a great, odd fleet of ships and boats. Some of the vessels were armed sailing ships. Some were whaleboats and Indian bark canoes. Many others were sturdy, weatherworn frontier boats called *bateaux*.

Bateaux were designed by frontiersmen and explorers for a specific purpose: to carry bulky supplies and bundles of animal skins for early American fur traders around the St. Lawrence River and the Great Lakes. Interestingly, these were the work boats developed and used by trappers from France—England's enemy!

question: Was Johnny too sure of himself in thinking he could win this campaign? He took for granted that he would sweep easily to Albany, shatter the rebellious colonists, and end the war. For the expedition southward, he packed 30 carts of personal belongings to keep himself comfortable. They included fine clothes, books, a rich store of wine, and other comforts. It seemed Johnny expected his great military adventure to be a grand party.

Perhaps he had good reason to be confident. He also was bringing with his army dozens of cannons, pulled by more than 200 horses. (Critics believed he was carrying far more cannons than he needed—which were bound to slow him down.) He intended to blast any enemy force he might find entrenched or secure behind fortress walls. It seemed nothing could stand against him.

In 1777, Johnny's army was large enough and experienced enough to frighten the enemy. He had more than 7,000 British regulars and German **mercenaries**, all experienced soldiers who could bear up to the hardships of the march and face enemy musket balls without being frightened. He also had several hundred Indian warriors and rugged Canadian settlers on his side.

They loaded their heavy cannons, livestock, and tons of supplies aboard freshwater transport vessels at St. Jean on the Richelieu River. The fleet spread for a mile along the river. On June 15, they sailed south toward Lake Champlain and Albany beyond. Johnny traveled aboard a schooner named the *Lady Maria*.

By late June, the fleet was past Valcour Island, where Carleton had been stalled the year before. It now was in the narrow lower regions of the lake, approaching Fort Ticonderoga, an American stronghold. Ticonderoga, commanded by Major General Arthur St. Clair, must be taken.

As he had learned at Breed's Hill two years before, Johnny intended to "soften" the Patriots' defenses with a ferocious cannon bombardment before sending in foot soldiers. He ordered his heavy artillery pieces hauled through the dense woods toward Fort Ticonderoga. This took days of hard work.

As it turned out, Fort Ticonderoga was easy to conquer—perhaps too easy. The Americans had only a third as many men as the British. Johnny's second-in-command, Major General William Phillips, secretly led an artillery unit to the top of Mt. Defiance, a peak that looked down into the fort. The Americans had not bothered to defend it because they believed it was too high and rugged for any enemy force to occupy. When the Americans saw to their astonishment that the British had taken the important high ground and were putting cannons in place, they slipped away by night. They left behind vast stores of much-needed supplies.

The British leaders in America and Britain had expected Fort Ticonderoga to be hard to capture. They had feared many of their soldiers would be killed in the assaut. When King George III received word of the easy victory weeks later, he could hardly believe it. "I have beat the

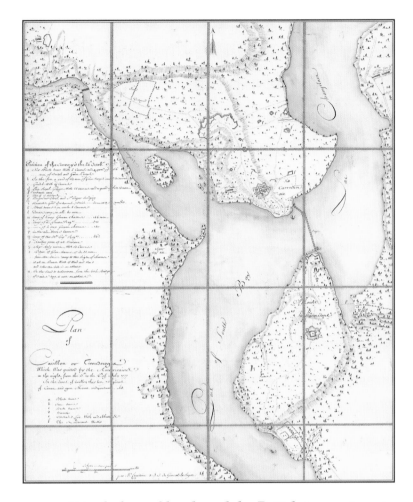

It took days of hard work by British troops to get their artillery in place around Fort Ticonderoga. The effort was rewarded with a victory for Johnny's troops.

Americans," he announced to the queen.

For the moment, Johnny was the toast of all England.

Johnny's men fought in a skirmish with American troops in Hubbardton, Vermont, in July 1777.

Serious Problems for the Invaders

The British occupied Fort Ticonderoga in 1777. They also won a follow-up skirmish at Hubbardton, Vermont, where Johnny's men chased and caught some of the Americans fleeing from Fort Ticonderoga. But at Hubbardton, there was fierce resistance from the Patriots. Johnny lost many men, and he lost time in his drive toward the south.

Things got even worse. Rather than follow the waterways, Johnny decided he could save time by going straight overland. To do that, work crews had to clear a new road through the woods wide enough for the artillery and the supply wagons. Workers labored in the muggy summer heat, batting mosquitoes. They had to cut away thousands of large trees the Americans felled to block their route. They had to build 40 bridges over streams and swampland. As a result, it took Johnny's army three weeks to travel just 23 miles.

Besides heat, mosquitoes, and backbreaking work, the soldiers had to beware of one particularly dangerous kind of foe in the wilderness. Lieutenant James M. Hadden, one of Johnny's artillery officers, kept a detailed journal of the campaign. He reported that one day "we saw and killed a great number of Rattle Snakes, in the Stomach of one of them we found two whole ground Squirrels. . . . This snake had 6 Rattles. One was killed which had 13 Rattles. . . . On an Island near this, an Artillery Man was stung to Death some years ago, and that Island is so famous for them as to be called Rattle Snake Island."

It was the end of July when Johnny finally got his troops and artillery through to Fort Edward, New York. He knew the rebel army from Fort Ticonderoga had retreated there, and yet Fort Edward was deserted when his force arrived.

Johnny's men were exhausted, so he paused at Fort Edward to give them a rest. At this point, the British began to lose the support of many settlers in the region who they expected to remain loyal to King George. The reason: murderous raids by the Indians who were England's allies. In one famous attack, the natives killed a young woman named Jane McCrea.

Killing any woman would have been a shock, but McCrea's murder was a disaster for the British. She was not a rebel colonist, but a Loyalist. She was engaged to a **Tory** officer and was visiting an elderly woman who was related to one of Johnny's own generals. Her death alarmed not only the local settlers, but also the British and Germans in Johnny's army.

Many of his officers never had approved of using the services of the unpredictable Indians. All along, the native warriors had been almost more troublesome than they were helpful. They didn't really like any white colonists— Loyalists or Patriots. These Canadian Indians agreed to help the British, but they didn't fully understand the reasons for the war. What they understood was that by joining Johnny's force, they might be able to drive away some of the white settlers.

At best, they were hard for Johnny to control. Lieutenant Hadden in July recorded: "The Savages getting drunk advanced too near the Enemy Lines, in the evening. This folly [ended] in an Officer being sent to bring them off. . . ." One Indian was killed. Another Indian and the British officer were wounded.

The British wanted the Indian allies to attack Patriot settlers, not settlers loyal to England. They expected the Indians to follow the accepted rules of war. In a speech before they

Johnny met with Canadian Indians to discuss their participation on the side of the British during the war.

began their expedition, Johnny had instructed the Indians: "Aged men, women, children, and prisoners must be held sacred from the knife or hatchet, even in the time of actual conflict."

The Indians had disobeyed. Furious, Johnny demanded that the warriors responsible be arrested and executed. The Indians' leader refused to turn the tribesmen over for trial. He warned Johnny that all the Indians would desert if McCrea's killers were punished. The general had to back down, after insisting that his orders be obeyed in the future.

Johnny did not realize it, but he was in for much worse trouble. In fact, his whole expedition might be doomed. The way events were falling into place, a large army of Americans—not the British led by Howe and the friendly Tories and Indians coming from the west with St. Leger—would be waiting for him as he approached Albany.

To the south, British General Howe was not doing what he was expected to do. Johnny thought Howe was marching his 15,000 soldiers up the Hudson River toward Albany. Instead, Howe placed much of his army aboard a great fleet of transport ships

British General Howe sent most of his army on ships sailing south to Philadelphia in an effort to capture the American capital. Johnny expected those troops to assist in the invasion of New York.

and sailed south down the Atlantic coast to capture the American capital, Philadelphia.

Howe was not really disobeying orders. The

orders Howe received from London weren't completely clear. As Howe understood it, he was not required to participate in Johnny's invasion plan, but was free to move his army into positions that he thought could do the most good.

When Johnny learned of Howe's plans, he was disturbed. Did Howe think Johnny's army alone could defeat the rebels in the upper colonies? Or did Howe believe that by taking Philadelphia he could persuade the colonists that continued fighting was pointless? This would make Howe–and Howe alone–the great British hero of the colonial rebellion. Whatever Howe was thinking, Johnny was abandoned to fend for himself.

In a way, though, Johnny was not too dismayed by Howe abandoning him. He believed he could smash the rebels in New York without Howe. If he could, then he rather than Howe would be the great hero.

But another disaster came in August. A

hundred miles to the west, his ally St. Leger was trying to reach Albany with a much smaller–but no less important–force of almost 2,000 men, half of them Indians. St. Leger was stalled trying to capture the American Fort Stanwix, an important frontier outpost on the Mohawk River, in New York State.

After days of siege, St. Leger's men defeated an American relief column at the village of Oriskany. St. Leger finally seemed on the verge of strangling the weakening American garrison at Fort Stanwix. But then he received word that an American army of 3,000 soldiers led by Major General Benedict Arnold was marching to rescue the fort.

Arnold had played a trick on St. Leger. He was coming–but with only 1,000 men, many of them inexperienced militia. But the Indians in the St. Leger's army believed the rumors Arnold's agents had spread about an American force three times its actual size. They deserted.

St. Leger had no choice but to withdraw and give up his march toward Albany. Many of his British and Hessian soldiers had been killed or wounded in skirmishes around Fort Stanwix, and the Americans had plundered their supplies.

This left Johnny alone to defeat the rebels in eastern New York. Yet, despite all the bad news, he still believed he could win. In a letter he wrote August 6, he told General Howe he expected to be in Albany easily before the end of the month.

He ordered a raid into Bennington, Vermont, to steal food, horses, and other goods for his army. The raiding force was led by one of his German dragoon commanders, Lieutenant Colonel Friedrich Baum, and consisted mostly of German mercenaries and Indians.

The Indians again proved to be unruly rather than helpful. They apparently did not understand the purpose of the mission. Rather than herding live cattle back to the main army to provide a lasting source of beef, they killed the cows, took their cowbells (which they prized very highly), and left the carcasses to rot. They also terrorized the settlers, adding to the anger that had been sparked by Jane McCrea's murder.

Then Baum's force ran into a trap. New Hampshire militia under General John Stark, some of them disguised as Loyalists, were waiting. The Patriots cut down hundreds of Baum's soldiers. Baum himself was killed. Lieutenant Colonel Heinrich von Breymann, who arrived with a unit of German reinforcements, was wounded. By nightfall, more than 200 Germans and Tories had died and 700 were prisoners of war. The Americans, who had suffered only 70 **casualties**, captured a valuable store of firearms and cannons.

Johnny's confidence now was shaken. Not only had he lost hundreds of men; the mission had failed to get any food, horses, or other

American Colonel Daniel Morgan, one of Johnny's foes in the fighting around Saratoga, was a giant among his men. He was six feet tall and strong as an ox, and he hated the British army.

Years before, Morgan had been a wagon driver for the redcoats during the French and Indian War. After an argument with a British officer, he had been punished with a ferocious, prolonged lashing that left his back permanently scarred. Those scars were a daily reminder of English brutality in the colonies.

Morgan's men fondly called him "the old wagoner." He was one of America's best leaders during the war. In early 1781, he whipped a force commanded by Britain's great cavalry officer, Lieutenant Colonel Banastre "Bloody Ban" Tarleton, at the Battle of Cowpens in South Carolina. Shortly afterward, Morgan was forced to retire because of bad health—but by then, the Revolution was almost won.

supplies for the army. In addition, the Americans who destroyed Baum's command were not uniformed veterans, but plainclothes militia—the kind of untrained fighters Johnny had predicted he easily would put down.

He desperately needed to persuade General Howe in New York to come to his aid, but he didn't even have a reliable way to communicate. His messengers carried coded memos hidden in their boot heels. Some were caught by American patrols, the papers discovered, the codes broken, and the messengers hanged. In a despairing letter to London, Johnny reported that "of the messengers I have sent, I know of two being hanged, and am ignorant whether any of the rest arrived."

With each passing day, "Gentleman Johnny" was feeling more and more cut off from the world.

Shown here is the left bank of the Hudson River, three miles above Stillwater.

Outnumbered at Saratoga

In September 1777, Johnny thought he finally would get a chance to confront (and, hopefully, defeat) the main American army in New York. American Major General Horatio Gates had entrenched his force near the Hudson River town of Stillwater. What Johnny may not have known was that Gates commanded a powerful army that was growing every day. Nearby settlers were inspired by the Bennington victory to take down their old hunting rifles and join the Patriot cause. At the same time, General George Washington to the south sent small but valuable units of veteran American soldiers to help Gates block Johnny's invasion.

The American commander was completely unlike Johnny Burgoyne. Johnny was dashing and handsome; Gates looked old and weak and wore funny eyeglasses (his own men called him "Granny"). Johnny was eager to fight; Gates was content to find good defensive ground and wait for the enemy's move. Johnny was willing to take chances in order to score impressive victories; Gates almost never acted if he saw any chance that something might go wrong.

By September 19, Johnny's redcoats had arrived near Stillwater and divided into three forces. Johnny himself commanded one large group. As his men marched across a clearing at Freeman's Farm, rifle fire cracked from the woods. In an instant, American sharpshooters struck down almost all the officers and many of the soldiers in Johnny's leading unit. The First Band of Freeman's Farm had begun.

Suddenly, the British were startled by a loud noise. It was not the firing of guns or the shouting of orders by enemy officers. It was something just as alarming but very, very strange on a battlefield: a turkey gobble! This was the way one of the American leaders, Colonel Daniel Morgan, had arranged to issue commands to his marksmen hiding in the woods. Morgan's wooden turkey call became a legend of the Revolutionary War.

The Americans did not form lines of battle and take turns with the enemy firing musket volleys–the way the British were accustomed to fighting. Instead, they hid behind trees and fired at will. Some of them even took to the treetops, from where they could fire clearly down into the British lines. Expert marksmen, they aimed for the British officers. With their superiors shot down, British soldiers fell into confusion.

Johnny himself had his coat and hat pierced by bullets during the battle. But he survived, boldly riding here and there amid the deafening, smoke-covered fighting to rally his troops.

Although American General Gates hesitated to engage Johnny's army in full combat, it

The British soldiers formed lines during battle, as shown here in this reenactment. They took turns with the enemy firing their muskets back and forth.

seemed Gates might win a decisive victory after all. His officers—bold leaders like Morgan and Arnold—were more than willing to fight, and so were his soldiers. They gave Johnny's proud army all it could handle.

At last, one of the other British forces joined

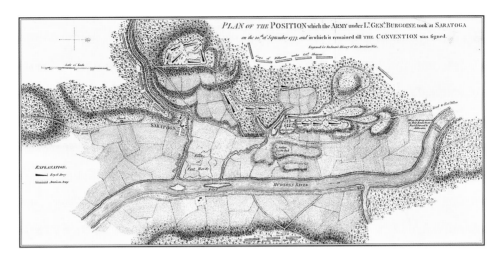

**This map details the Battle of Saratoga, where
American General Horatio Gates trapped and
attacked Johnny's troops.**

Johnny's men, and the Americans were forced
to withdraw. Johnny held the battlefield at the
end of the day, but he had lost more than 600
soldiers, compared to 300 American casualties.

He realized now that his army was in trouble.
While no decisive battles had been fought, he had
suffered heavy losses. It was difficult and dangerous for his men to obtain food and other provi-
sions. Instead of finding the countryside filled with
British sympathizers who would help them, they
found a growing army of American regulars and

militia who smelled victory over the hated British army. Johnny had hoped for reinforcements, but it was becoming clear help would not arrive.

With autumn, the weather was turning chilly and rainy. It was not easy to light campfires with wet wood. The British soldiers were miserable in their wet uniforms. About 800 ill and wounded men suffered in crude field shelters that had to serve as hospitals. Wolves howled threateningly from the dark woods at night. American riflemen and patrols picked off guards at British outposts and captured isolated redcoat parties out foraging for food. The proud English and Germans didn't have much to eat, and their meals always consisted of plain, salted pork and water. Many soldiers deserted—a military crime punished by hanging or unbearable lashing. Johnny knew his army could not stay here.

On October 7, the British and Americans clashed again near Freeman's Farm. The British commander again defied danger, riding through the thick of the shooting and smoke. At one point his horse was shot from under him.

Johnny escaped injury, but at this battle, one of his most valuable officers and closest friends, General Simon Fraser, was among the officers fatally wounded. In a furious series of attacks and a withering display of sharpshooting, the Americans threw Johnny's army into confusion.

Fraser wasn't the only important officer Johnny lost in that battle. Lieutenant Colonel Heinrich von Breymann, who had led the German reinforcements at Bennington, flew into a rage at his own men when they fled from the

Timothy Murphy was an amazing hero of the Revolutionary War. He was a New Jersey frontiersman who went north with Daniel Morgan's riflemen to join the fight.

Among Murphy's most famous deeds was capturing an officer from the center of the British camp. He and his friend David Elerson took one of Burgoyne's picket guards by surprise one night and made the soldier reveal the camp's password. Murphy then went alone among the British campfires, where the enemy troops thought he must be a Tory. Murphy silently crept into the tent of an officer and at bayonet point, Murphy forced the redcoat to go with him silently back to the American lines.

Not long afterward, Johnny's finest officer, General Simon Fraser, was killed at the Second Battle of Freeman's Farm. It was the deciding moment in Johnny's losing campaign. Some historians believe Timothy Murphy was the marksman who fired the fatal bullet.

**Timothy Murphy, a frontiersman, fought
for independence.**

battlefield. He slashed at his retreating soldiers with
his sword to try to stop their retreat. In fear and
fury, they shot him down and continued to run.

Johnny was more than relieved when night
came and the rebels broke off the fighting. He
had lost almost 800 more men.

He ordered his army to pull back a few miles up the Hudson to Saratoga. There, they were somewhat secure, but stuck. More Patriot militia arrived. Hordes of Americans surrounded the great British army and intercepted incoming supplies. Johnny, always the well-dressed dandy, now had to endure more than two weeks without changing his bullet-torn clothes. Many of his men were in far worse condition.

By now, Gates' American forces numbered some 18,000–three times the size of Johnny's shrinking army. Gates had the redcoats surrounded. The only thing preventing the Patriots from attacking and destroying the British was Gates' dread of fighting.

Perhaps it was just as well. There was no need for an infantry attack, which would result in much bloodshed on both sides. The Americans could simply pound Johnny's Saratoga entrenchments with cannons from a distance, and wait for the British to starve or surrender.

Johnny surrendered the British troops to American General Gates at Saratoga in October 1777.

6

Return to the Gentleman's Life

It was clear to almost everyone that Johnny's army and military career were doomed. Yet, he was the tireless merrymaker even in the final days of the failed Saratoga campaign. He settled in at a Tory's mansion and proceeded to have parties. "While the army was suffering from cold and hunger," wrote one of his critics in amazement, " . . . [the] house was illuminated, and rung with singing, laughter, and the jingling of glasses. There Burgoyne was sitting, with some merry companions, at a dainty supper, while the **champagne** was flowing."

Soon enough, Johnny had to face reality. It was now

a simple choice of life or death. Johnny chose life for himself and his army. On October 13, he began negotiating terms for his men to lay down their weapons.

American General Gates was very nervous. He was afraid another British army might come up from New York and attack the rear of his army. He was so happy that the fighting around Saratoga was ending that he granted practically all Johnny's requests in ending the campaign. The British and German soldiers were not to be taken prisoners of war, but were to be marched to Boston, fed along the way by the Americans. From there, they were to be shipped back to England, as long as they promised not to fight again in the colonies. Johnny and his officers could keep their lavish baggage. The agreement wasn't called a "surrender"; a much gentler term was stated in the official record: "convention."

In short, Johnny didn't officially surrender his army; he merely surrendered their weapons. His men, Gates agreed, would be taken to the coast and from there would be free to go home. It was almost as if Johnny had won and Gates had lost, or at worst, as if the two sides had agreed to a draw.

Looking back, though, there is no doubt who lost. In the fighting around Saratoga, 1,400 redcoats were killed or wounded. The rest–almost 5,000– were taken prisoner. The Patriots took over all their weapons and supplies, including 27 badly needed cannons. Johnny lost his entire army.

Many Revolutionary War historians believe that it was here that England basically lost the war. Among other long-term results, the Americans'

British General Howe's decision in New York City not to send a large army up the Hudson River to join Johnny's force led to the surrender at Saratoga. Johnny's men, left alone, eventually were surrounded by thousands of American militia and were starved into surrendering.

Instead General Howe sent his men down the coast to capture Philadelphia, the American capital at the time. Howe believed this would break up the American Revolution. Instead, it bogged down his British army, which was trying to catch George Washington's ragged, weary force. And it made the citizens of Pennsylvania very angry. Rather than become Loyalists and help the British, as Howe had expected, many of them supported Washington's American army.

victory at Saratoga persuaded France to join them and help defeat the British.

A few days after the surrender, Johnny wrote a letter to his nieces in England. He talked of the "personal hazard" he had endured. "I have been surrounded with enemies, ill-treated by pretended friends, abandoned by a considerable part of my own army, totally unassisted by Sir William Howe," he complained. He added that he was "under perpetual fire, and exhausted with laborious days, and 16 almost sleepless nights, without change of clothes, or other covering than the sky. I have been with my army within the jaws of famine; shot through my hat and waistcoat, my nearest friends killed round me. . . ."

In the end, the British did not receive the easy treatment Johnny and General Gates had agreed to. They were held at Boston over the winter. Then Congress decided they should be moved to a Virginia prison camp. Johnny's soldiers spent the rest of the war in miserable confinement there. By the war's end, most of them had died of sickness.

General Gates, shown here, had reached an agreement with Johnny following his surrender. But the American Congress refused to go along with the plan.

Does this mean Congress violated the surrender terms agreed to by Johnny and Gates at Saratoga? It would seem that way. Some historians point out, though, that British General Howe secretly planned to send Johnny's released soldiers right back into service in the lower colonies. Even if the defeated troops actually sailed home to

England, they quickly would have been assigned to England's other army outposts around the world. British soldiers already stationed in those places then would have been sent to America to fight. So within months, all the "losses" England suffered by surrendering at Saratoga would have been replaced. Gates' victory would have been worthless to America.

The British commander sailed home on parole soon after the new year began. Johnny was free, but he knew he never again would find military glory. He asked the government to hold an official **court-martial** so he could explain, in his own way, why the Saratoga campaign had failed. No court-martial ever was held.

Back in America, the Patriots laughingly added a new verse about Johnny's defeat to their famous tune "Yankee Doodle":

In vain they fought; in vain they fled,
  Their Chief, humane and tender,
To save the rest, he thought it best,
  His Forces to surrender.

Musicians played "Yankee Doodle" with an added verse about Johnny's defeat.

Many citizens and government leaders in England, too, criticized Johnny for his great loss in America. The military leaders in London did not treat him too harshly, though. A few years later, he was named commander in chief of British forces in Ireland.

After a year there, he returned to London. Johnny still was involved in government—he was a member of Parliament until his death. But for the most part, he settled back into the easy life of high society. He loved the latest fashions, expensive dinners, entertainment—especially theater—and all the other fine things in life.

Soon, he was famous not only as an army general, but as a playwright. Several of his plays were published and performed on the London stage. His best-known work is titled *The Heiress*. It was performed in Drury Lane, a London district famous for its theaters, and later in Germany and France.

Johnny was afraid his war career was influencing the opinions of theatergoers when they went to see his plays performed. If they admired his military record, they likely would find something to enjoy in his plays. If they scorned him because of his loss at Saratoga, they would tend to criticize his writings, no matter how good.

To learn what people truly thought of his work, he crafted a new play titled *Lord of the Manor* and did not put his name on it. He was delighted when the critics began guessing who had written the play. They agreed it was a fine achievement and guessed it was written by one or another of the best playwrights of the day—all of whom had to admit they were not the authors. "Gentleman Johnny" Burgoyne had proved his talent as a man of literature, beyond any challenge.

As he entered old age, Johnny had four children outside of marriage. The oldest, a son named John, was born in 1782. The boy grew to earn his own reputation as an army officer. Eventually, Sir John Fox Burgoyne would be knighted by the queen and made a field marshal of the British army.

The younger John Burgoyne was still a boy when his father died. "Gentleman Johnny," the dandy soldier and statesman who had tasted both glory and defeat, died of a disease called **gout** in 1792. He was 70. His body was laid to rest at Westminster Abbey in London.

GLOSSARY

artillery–cannons, mortars, and other heavy guns in an army.

casualties–soldiers killed or injured in battle.

champagne–a kind of alcoholic drink usually served at special celebrations.

civilian–a person in wartime who is not a member of the armed forces.

colony–a foreign territory that a country controls and governs.

commission–in armies and navies of the 18th century, a government paper naming an officer to a particular rank.

court-martial–a military trial to decide whether an officer or soldier/sailor was at personal fault in the loss of a battle or in failing to carry out orders.

dragoon–a heavily armed soldier on horseback.

gout–a painful disease of the joints.

Hessian–a soldier from the German state of Hesse who fought for England in the American Revolution.

homespun–simple, homemade clothes and tools used by settlers.

invade–to send an army into a foreign land.

Loyalist–an American colonist who remained loyal to King George III of England during the Revolution.

mercenary–a soldier who fights–usually for another country– for money or other rewards, not out of a sense of duty or respect.

militia–a group of citizens who agree to arm themselves and fight in times of emergency, usually for only a short period of weeks or months.

Parliament–the British governing body, consisting of a House of Commons and House of Lords.

parole–the release of a prisoner under certain conditions.

Patriot– a person who faithfully supports his or her country even in times of trouble.

playwright–a person who writes plays.

redcoats–name for 18th-century British soldiers, most of whom wore bright red jackets.

schooner–a type of sailing vessel.

siege–the surrounding of an enemy stronghold for an extended period, cutting it off from retreat or from relief from the outside.

skirmish–a brief conflict between small groups of opposing soldiers in a war.

Tory– a supporter of England in the American colonies; also called a Loyalist.

CHRONOLOGY

1722 John ("Gentleman Johnny") Burgoyne is born near London, England, on February 4.

1737 Joins the British Army at age 15.

1743 Runs away with Charlotte Stanley, daughter of the Earl of Derby, to get married.

1756 Becomes a captain in the 11th Royal Dragoons.

1761 Elected to the British Parliament while home on leave from the army.

1762 Leads a force that captures the Portuguese town of Valencia d'Alcántara during the Seven Years' War. He is rewarded by the King of Portugal and becomes a hero in England.

1775 Goes to America as a major general in the army. He takes part in the fighting around Boston, including the Battle of Bunker Hill.

1776 Spends the winter at home on leave, then returns to North America to take part in the first British invasion of the New York colony from Canada.

1777 Leads the second invasion of New York from Canada. The campaign ends in his army's surrender at Saratoga.

1778 Returns to England; takes his seat in Parliament; and resumes his career as a playwright.

1782 Begins a short term as commander in chief of British forces in Ireland.

1792 Suffering from painful gout, he dies in London.

REVOLUTIONARY WAR TIME LINE ═══

1765   The Stamp Act is passed by the British. Violent protests against it break out in the colonies.

1766   Britain ends the Stamp Act.

1767   Britain passes a law that taxes glass, painter's lead, paper, and tea in the colonies.

1770   Five colonists are killed by British soldiers in the Boston Massacre.

1773   People are angry about the taxes on tea. They throw boxes of tea from ships in Boston harbor into the water. It ruins the tea. The event is called the Boston Tea Party.

1774   The British pass laws to punish Boston for the Boston Tea Party. They close Boston harbor. Leaders in the colonies meet to plan a response to these actions.

1775   The battles of Lexington and Concord begin the American Revolution.

1776   The Declaration of Independence is signed. France and Spain give money to help the Americans fight Britain. Nathan Hale is captured by the British. He is charged with being a spy and is executed.

1777   Leaders choose a flag for America. The American troops win some important battles over the British. General Washington and his troops spend a very cold, hungry winter in Valley Forge.

1778 France sends ships to help the Americans win the war. The British are forced to leave Philadelphia.

1779 French ships head back to France. The French support the Americans in other ways.

1780 Americans discover that Benedict Arnold is a traitor. He escapes to the British. Major battles take place in North and South Carolina.

1781 The British surrender at Yorktown.

1783 A peace treaty is signed in France. British troops leave New York.

1787 The U.S. Constitution is written. Delaware becomes the first state in the Union.

1789 George Washington becomes the first president. John Adams is vice president.

FURTHER READING

Cumming, William P., & Hugh F. Rankin. *The Fate of a Nation: The American Revolution Through Contemporary Eyes.* London: Phaidon Press Limited, 1975.

Garrison, Webb. *Great Stories of the American Revolution.* Nashville, TN: Rutledge Hill Press, 1990.

Hall, Jonathan N. *Revolutionary War Quiz & Fact Book.* Dallas, TX: Taylor Publishing Company, 1999.

Kelly, C. Brian, et al. *Best Little Stories From the American Revolution.* Nashville, TN: Cumberland House, 1999.

Ketchum, Richard M. *Saratoga: Turning Point of America's Revolutionary War.* New York: Henry Holt & Company, 1997.

Masoff, Joy. *American Revolution: 1700-1800.* New York: Scholastic Inc., 2000.

Murray, Stuart. *The Honor of Command: General Burgoyne's Saratoga Campaign.* Bennington, VT: Images From the Past, Inc., 1998.

INDEX

PICTURE CREDITS

ABOUT THE AUTHOR

DANIEL E. HARMON of Spartanburg, South Carolina, has writtenwritten 29 books and numerous articles on topics ranging from history to humor. He is the editor of *The Lawyer's PC,* a national computer newsletter, and associate editor of *Sandlapper: The Magazine of South Carolina.*

Senior Consulting Editor **ARTHUR M. SCHLESINGER, JR.** is the leading American historian of our time. He won the Pulitzer Prize for his book *The Age of Jackson* (1945), and again for *A Thousand Days* (1965). This chronicle of the Kennedy Administration also won a National Book Award. He has written many other books, including a multi-volume series, *The Age of Roosevelt.* Professor Schlesinger is the Albert Schweitzer Professor of the Humanities at the City University of New York, and has been involved in several other Chelsea House projects, including the Colonial Leaders series of biographies on the most prominent figures of early American history.